AF364905

THE ULTIMATE

Wolf

BOOK *for* KIDS

Copyright © 2024 by Jenny Kellett
Wolves: The Ultimate Wolf Book for Kids

www.bellanovabooks.com

All rights reserved. No part of this book may be reproduced in any form by any electronic or mechanical means including photocopying, recording, or information storage and retrieval without permission in writing from the author.

Imprint: Bellanova Books

Contents

Introduction

WELCOME TO THE WILD WORLD OF WOLVES!

Wolves are fascinating creatures that have captured the imagination of people for centuries. But what exactly is a wolf, and what makes them so special? Let's embark on an adventure to learn all about these incredible animals.

WHAT IS A WOLF?

Wolves are not just the stuff of fairy tales; they are real, living animals that belong to the dog family, Canidae. They are known for their sharp teeth, strong bodies, keen senses, and, most importantly, their ability to work together as a team.

Wolves don't actually howl at the moon—this is just a myth!

Let's meet the Canidae Family

Wolves are part of a big family called Canidae, which includes all sorts of dogs, from domestic pets to wild species like coyotes and foxes. Canids are found on all continents in the world, except for Antarctica.

Maned wolf

Despite its appearance and name, the maned wolf is neither a wolf nor a fox!

Arctic fox

The Arctic fox is a small, fluffy predator that lives in the icy Arctic. Its white coat helps it blend into the snowy landscape.

African wild dog

Jackel

Jackals are the clever scavengers of the savanna, mostly found in Africa and southern parts of Asia.

African wild dogs, also known as painted wolves, have colorful, patchy coats that are different on every single one!

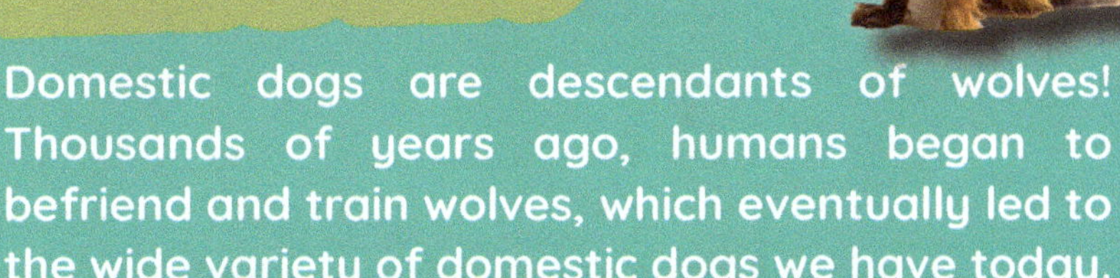

Domestic dogs are descendants of wolves! Thousands of years ago, humans began to befriend and train wolves, which eventually led to the wide variety of domestic dogs we have today.

Strong snout
Just like dogs, wolves have an amazing sense of smell!
Acute ears
Their upright ears help them to hear every whisper in the forest!
Sharp teeth
Wolves' sharp teeth help them grip and tear meat.
Tough paws
Their paws help them grip onto tough terrains, from snowy hills to rocky paths.

Wolf Anatomy

Wolves are designed for **survival**. Their strong legs help them travel long distances, their fur keeps them warm in cold climates, and their sharp senses help them track down food.

Thick fur

Wolves have a special layer of fur that keeps them warm in the winter.

Bushy tail

Their bushy tails are used to help them balance and also for communicating with other wolves.

Strong legs

Their muscular legs help them to leap and sprint through the forest.

The Life of a Wolf

Ever wondered what a day in the life of a wolf looks like? Wolves lead fascinating lives filled with hunting, playing, and roaming across vast landscapes. In this chapter, we'll explore how wolves live, hunt, and communicate within their packs.

DID YOU KNOW?
The red wolf (pictured) is also known as 'America's Wolf' because it's the only wolf that only lives in the USA - and nowhere else.

A Day in the Life of a Wolf

Wolves have busy lives! From the moment they wake up, wolves are on the move, exploring their territories, playing with pack members, or resting together.

Wolves are very adaptable and may hunt or play at different times of day depending on the weather or availability of prey.

Resting

After a busy night of activity, wolves often rest during the day. They might find a shaded area in their territory to sleep and conserve energy.

Socializing

Afternoons and evenings are often for playing in their packs!

Hunting

Nighttime is prime hunting time for wolves due to their nocturnal prey. However, they may hunt at other times, too!

Where Wolves Roam and Rest
Territories vs Dens
DID YOU KNOW?
Wolves don't use just one den! They often have multiple dens within their territory and will move their pups if danger lurks too close!

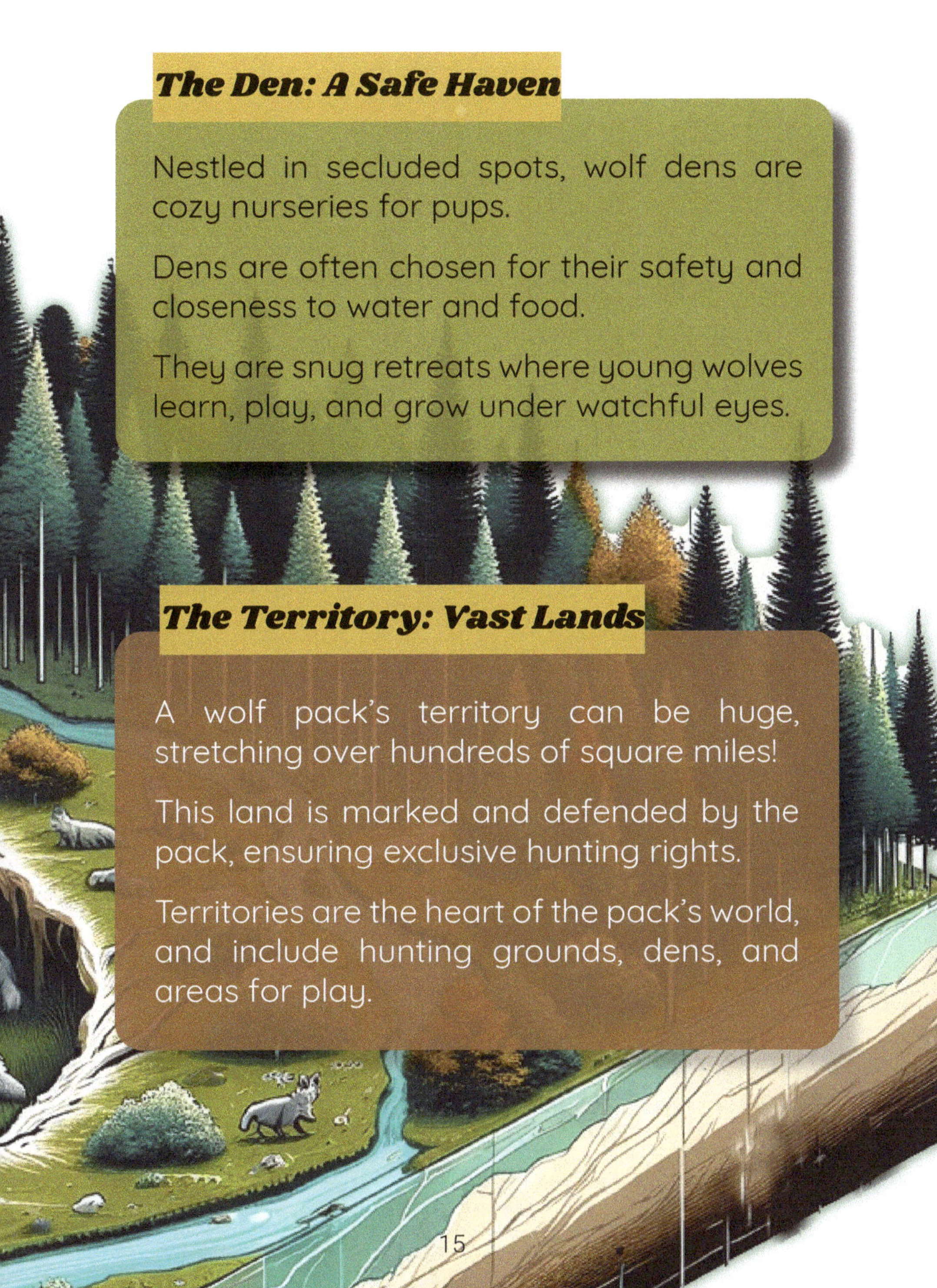

The Den: A Safe Haven

Nestled in secluded spots, wolf dens are cozy nurseries for pups.

Dens are often chosen for their safety and closeness to water and food.

They are snug retreats where young wolves learn, play, and grow under watchful eyes.

The Territory: Vast Lands

A wolf pack's territory can be huge, stretching over hundreds of square miles!

This land is marked and defended by the pack, ensuring exclusive hunting rights.

Territories are the heart of the pack's world, and include hunting grounds, dens, and areas for play.

The Wolf Pack

In a wolf pack, there's a strict hierarchy, with an alpha male and female leading the group. These leaders make decisions, like when and where to hunt. But every wolf, from the strongest to the youngest pup, has an important role in the pack.

THE ALPHA PAIR

The alpha male and female are the leaders of the pack. They are usually the parents of most of the pack's members and make important decisions, such as when to hunt, where to travel, and where to den. The alpha pair has the exclusive right to breed within the pack.

THE BETA WOLVES

These are the second in command and are often the enforcers of the alpha's decisions. They help maintain order and discipline within the pack, and if the alphas are busy, the betas may take temporary leadership.

THE HUNTERS

The hunters are usually skilled adult wolves. They take part in hunts and are often the most experienced members when it comes to finding prey.

These wolves
do lots of
different
jobs, from
helping out
with the hunt to
babysitting the
pups.

THE OMEGA WOLVES

These are the lowest-ranking members of the pack and often act as the 'scapegoats' if there is any aggression. Despite their low status, omegas play an important social role, often initiating play and helping to solve conflicts within the pack.

Wolf pups are the future of the pack. While they are not involved in hunting, all members help protect and educate them.

These wise old wolves may not run with the hunt, but they have plenty of know-how to share. They look after the pups and help keep the den safe, using their wisdom to guide the pack.

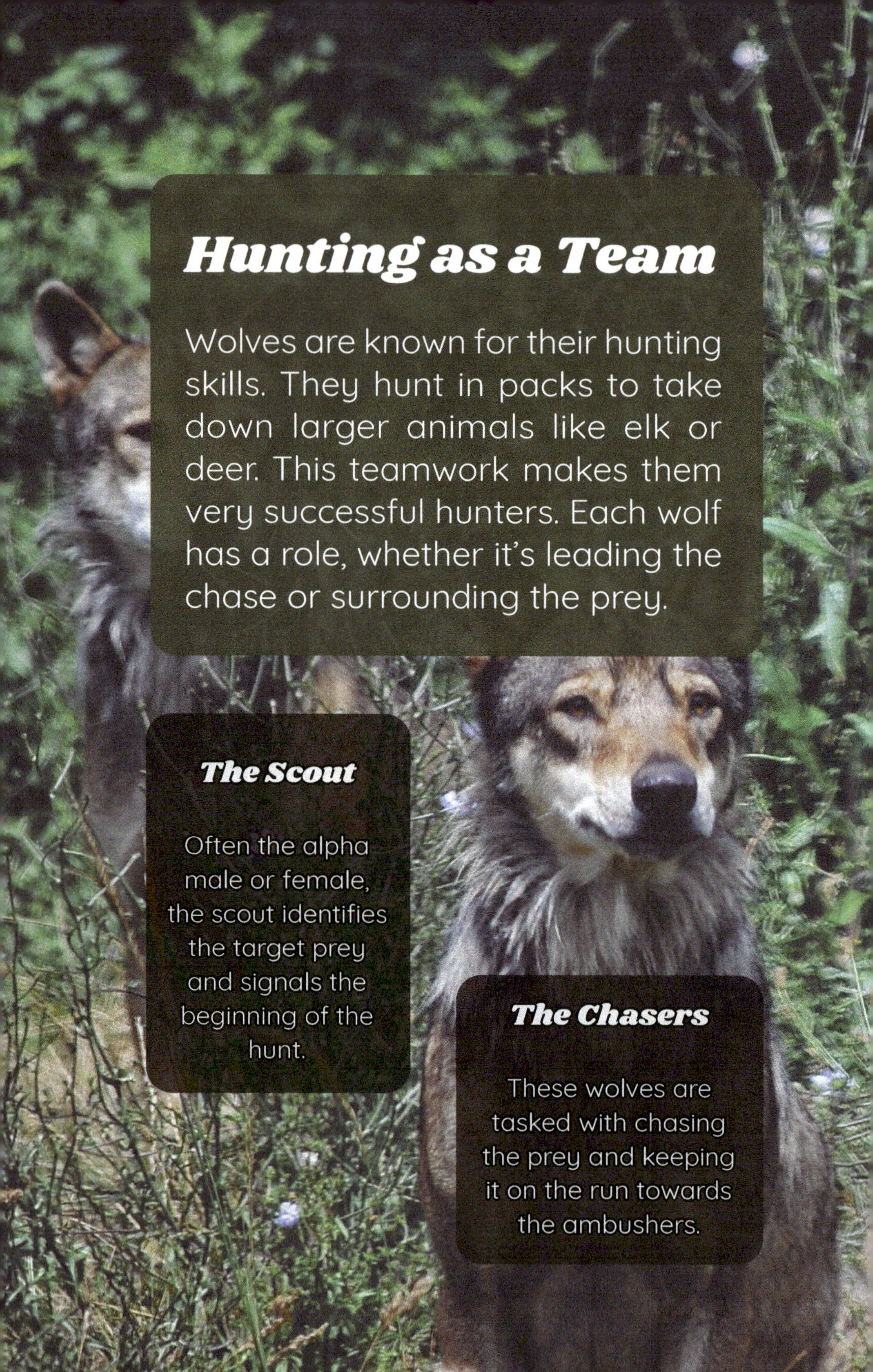

Hunting as a Team

Wolves are known for their hunting skills. They hunt in packs to take down larger animals like elk or deer. This teamwork makes them very successful hunters. Each wolf has a role, whether it's leading the chase or surrounding the prey.

The Scout

Often the alpha male or female, the scout identifies the target prey and signals the beginning of the hunt.

The Chasers

These wolves are tasked with chasing the prey and keeping it on the run towards the ambushers.

In a hunt, wolves take on roles that best suit their skills and the needs of the pack at that moment— their roles can always change.

The Ambushers

They lie in wait, hidden from the prey until the chasers bring it to them.

The Finishers

Once the prey is exhausted and cornered by the chasers and ambushers, the finishers move in to make the final takedown.

The Supporters

These are often younger or less dominant wolves that help in the hunt as needed and learn from the expert wolves.

Talk of the Pack

Wolves have their own language! They communicate through howls, barks, growls, and body language. This helps them stay connected with their pack and warn off other animals.

A wolf's famous howl can tell other wolves where it is, call the pack back together, or warn strangers to keep out of their home turf.

A wolf's tail can say so many things! A high, wagging tail might mean happiness, while a tucked tail could be a sign of worry.

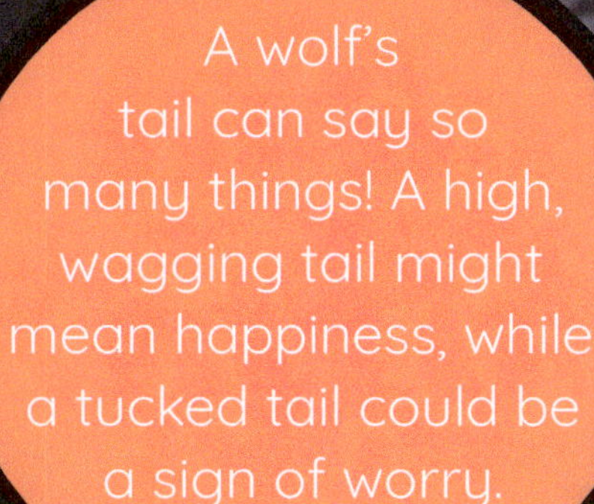

DID YOU KNOW?

Wolves' howls can be heard over 10 miles away in open terrain!

Wolves have super expressive faces. They use their ears, eyes, and even teeth to show if they're feeling friendly or if it's time to back off.

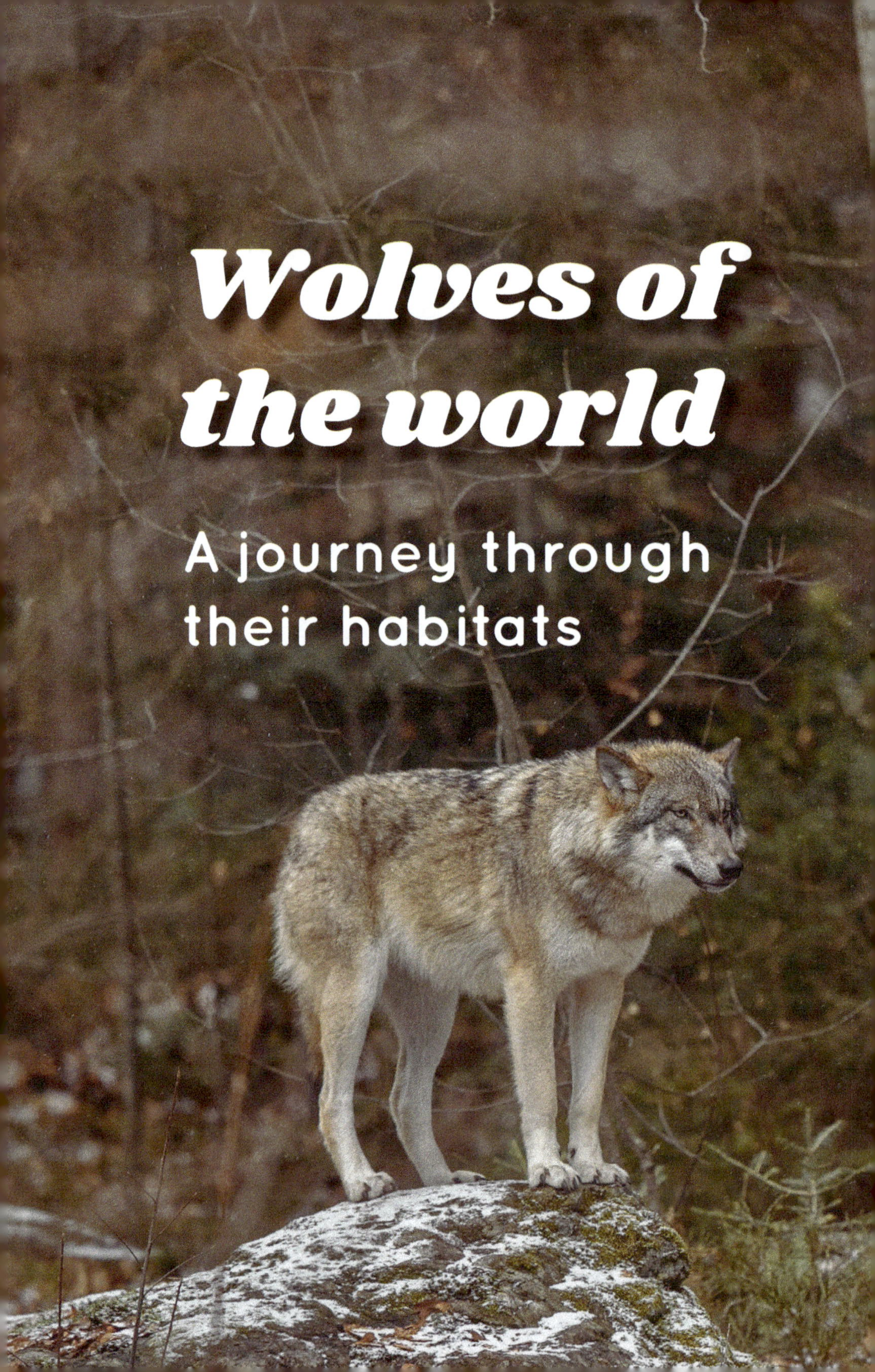

Wolves of the world
A journey through their habitats

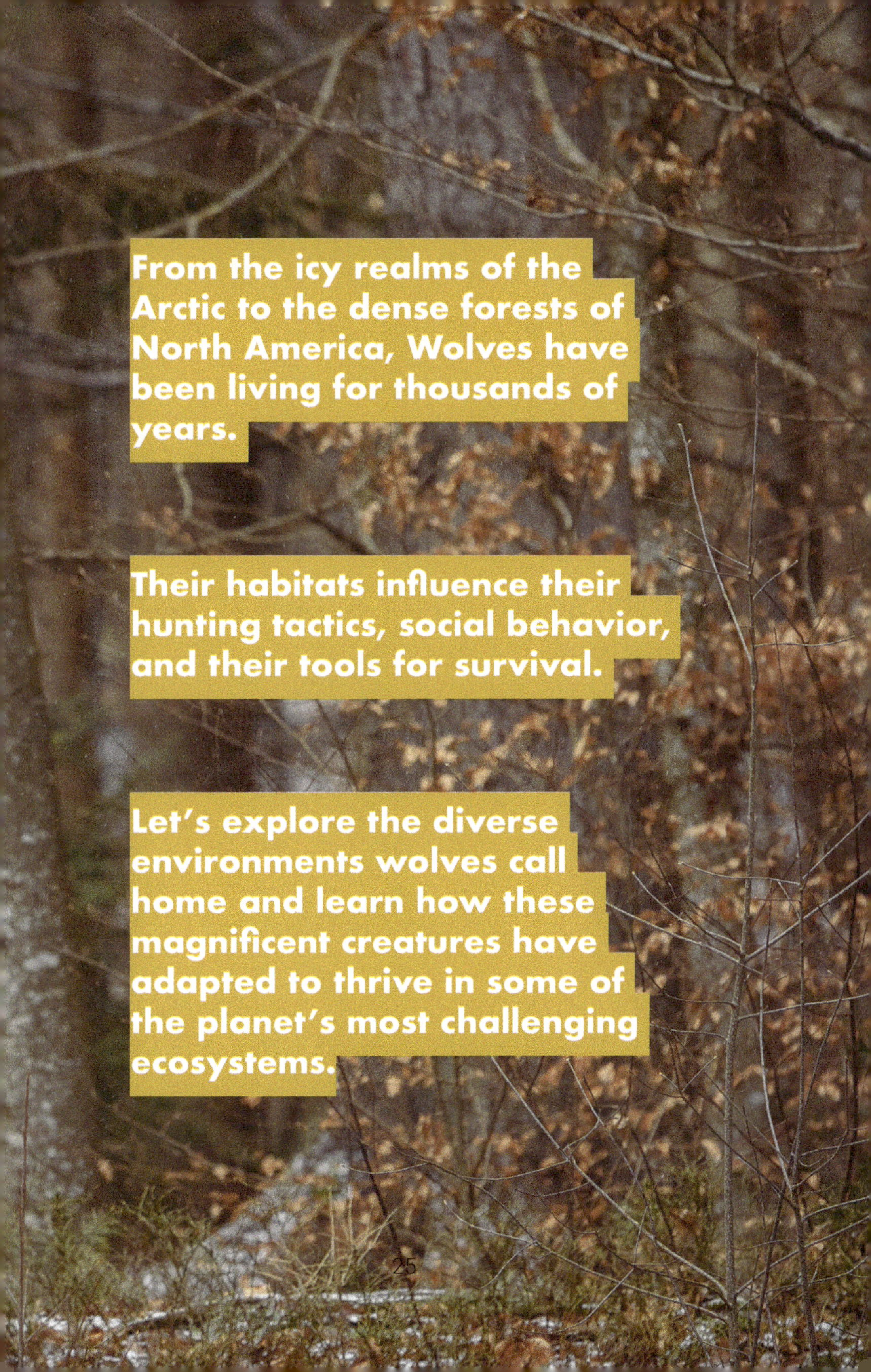
From the icy realms of the Arctic to the dense forests of North America, Wolves have been living for thousands of years.

Their habitats influence their hunting tactics, social behavior, and their tools for survival.

Let's explore the diverse environments wolves call home and learn how these magnificent creatures have adapted to thrive in some of the planet's most challenging ecosystems.

Where do wolves live?!

Wolves live all over the world - on all continents except Antarctica and Australia! Do you know which species live closest to you?!

Himalayan wolf
Eurasian wolf
Europe
Asia
Africa
Indian Ocean
African wolf
DID YOU KNOW?
There are no wolf species native to Australia or South America! The **maned wolf** of South America and the **dingo** of Australia are very close relatives, though.
27

The Arctic Wolf

Arctic wolves survive in some of the world's harshest conditions.

Can you imagine living in -30°F? That's where the Arctic wolf calls home! Most arctic wolves live in Alaska and northern Canada.

SURVIVAL SECRETS

- They wear a thick fur coat that's like a super-warm blanket, even when it's way below zero!

- Their **small ears and short noses** are great at keeping the heat in!

- They have built-in snow boots! Their **furry feet** let them sneak up on their prey without a sound.

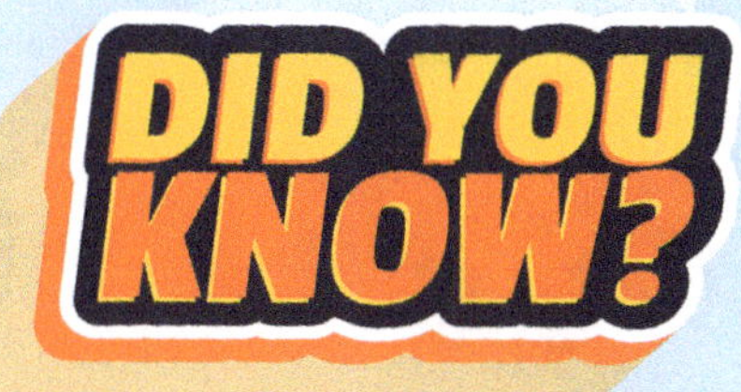

The Arctic wolf is one of the many cousins of the gray wolf, and it has adapted to live in places where most other animals can't survive!

DIET

- Muskoxen, caribou, and Arctic hares are their favorite food.

- They use their **strong sense of smell** to find prey underneath the snow.

- They don't need to eat every day thanks to their ability to **save energy** for weeks!

Mountain Wolves

Could you survive on a mountain?! Some wolf species, like the Himalayan wolf and northern Rocky Mountain wolf, thrive in mountain areas! These wolves are skilled navigators of steep, rocky slopes, living in some of the most breathtaking yet challenging terrains on Earth.

SURVIVAL SECRETS

- Mountain wolves' paws are larger than their cousins', giving them a better grip on snowy slopes.

- They have strong leg muscles, perfect for leaping between rocks and climbing steep cliffs.

- In the rugged mountains, these wolves prefer smaller packs for easier maneuvering and efficient hunting.

HIMALAYAN WOLF

Scientific name: Canis lupus chanco

Habitat: Himalayan Mountains

Weight: 70-120 lbs (32-54 kg)

Diet: Wild goats, sheep, small rodents.

NORTHERN ROCKY MOUNTAIN WOLF

Scientific name: Canis lupus irremotus

Habitat: Rocky Mountains, USA & Canada

Weight: 79-145 lbs (36-66 kg)

Diet: Moose, bison, elk, caribou, sheep, deer, mountain goats.

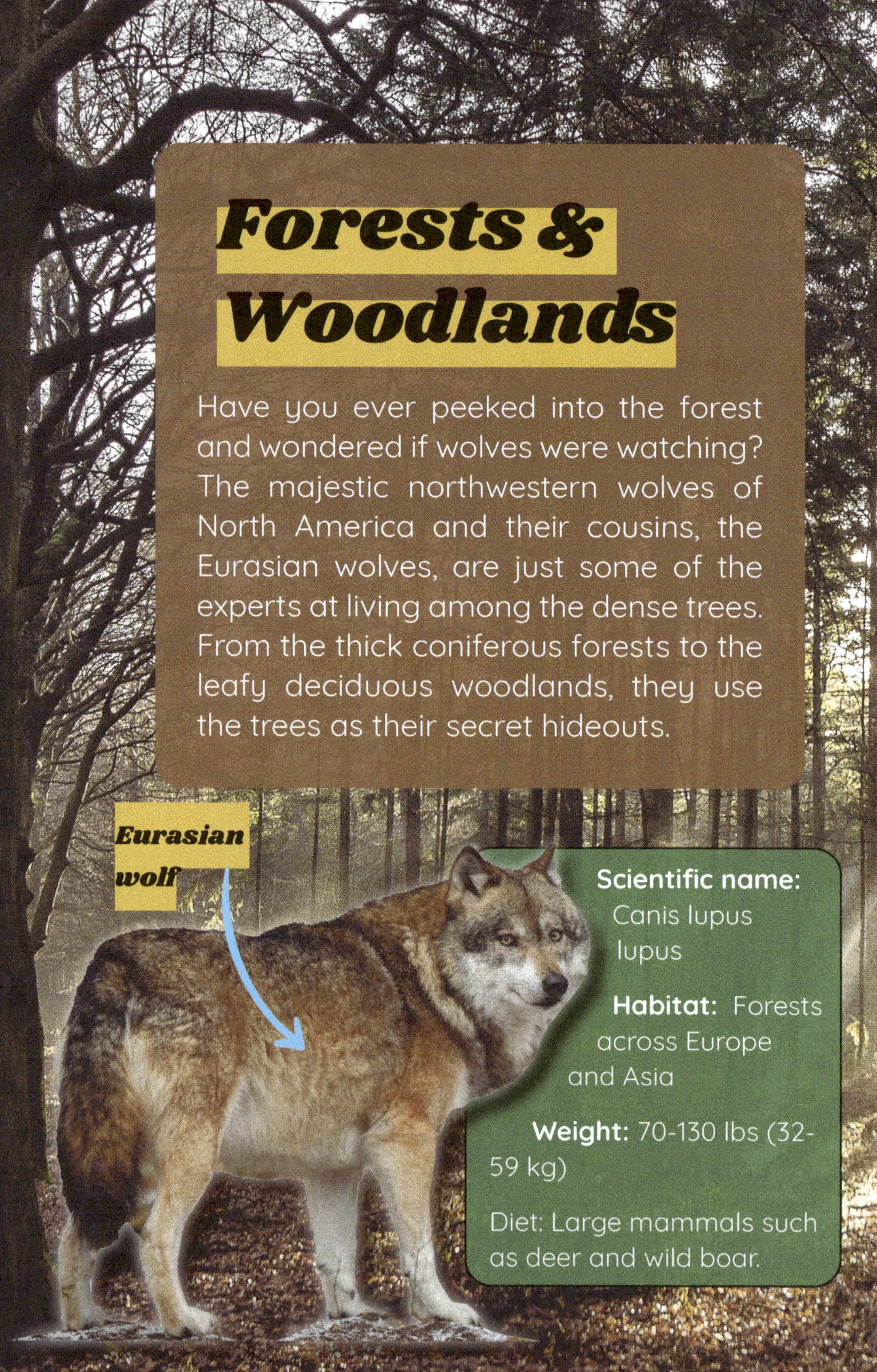

Forests & Woodlands

Have you ever peeked into the forest and wondered if wolves were watching? The majestic northwestern wolves of North America and their cousins, the Eurasian wolves, are just some of the experts at living among the dense trees. From the thick coniferous forests to the leafy deciduous woodlands, they use the trees as their secret hideouts.

Eurasian wolf

Scientific name: Canis lupus lupus

Habitat: Forests across Europe and Asia

Weight: 70-130 lbs (32-59 kg)

Diet: Large mammals such as deer and wild boar.

?

Most of the world's wolves live in forests. Do you know why? These dense habitats offer them plenty of cover and a diverse diet, making it a prime location for these expert hunters to thrive!

Scientific name: Canis lupus occidentalis

Habitat: Dense forests and open woodlands of northwestern North America.

Weight: 85-155 lbs (38-70 kg)

Diet: Large mammals such as elk, deer and moose.

Northwestern wolf

Desert Wolves

Did you know that wolves can also live in deserts?! Despite extreme temperatures and little water or prey, special wolf species such as the Arabian wolf have adapted to make the desert their unlikely home.

SURVIVAL SECRETS

- With smaller, leaner bodies, desert wolves need less water to stay hydrated and can go longer without drinking.

- They have light-colored fur that reflects the sun's rays and a thinner undercoat, making it easier to live in a hot climate.

- Arabian wolves are **opportunistic feeders** with stealthy hunting skills, which means they can catch quick prey like rodents and birds.

The Arabian wolf is the smallest wolf species in the world.

Scientific name: Canis lupus arabs

Habitat: Arabian Peninsula, including desert areas in countries like Saudi Arabia, Oman, Yemen, Jordan, and Israel.

Weight: 40-55 lbs (18 to 25 kg)

Diet: Their diet includes hares, rodents, birds, and carrion.

Diet & Hunting

Wolves are **carnivores**, meaning they eat meat. So how do they get their meat? Well, by hunting of course! Wolves are skilled hunters that use a variety of tactics to catch their prey. Let's find out more!

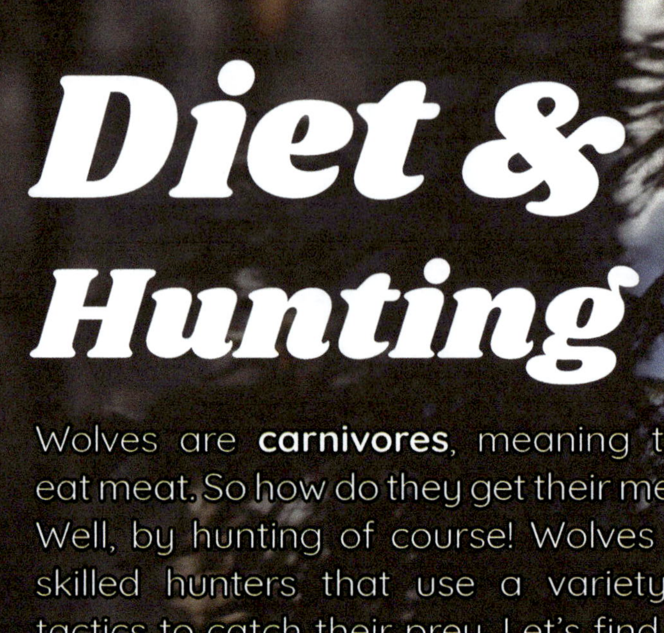

Wolves in the Food Chain

Wolves sit at the top of the food chain, which means they play a very important role in keeping the ecosystem balanced.

By hunting, wolves control the population of **herbivores**, such as rabbits, giving plants a chance to thrive. This benefits the whole ecosystem from the ground up!

Wolves not only control the herbivore population but also help in seed dispersal! As wolves roam, the seeds of various plants stick to their fur and get scattered across different areas, helping in the growth of new plants.

The Energy Starter
The sun provides energy to plants, which are the first step in the food chain.

The Producers
Plants use sunlight to grow and are eaten by many animals.

The Predator
Wolves eat animals like rabbits to get their energy and help keep the population in check.

The Plant Eaters
Herbivores eat plants to get their energy.

Can you think of another predator that plays a key role in the food chain?

The Recyclers
Tiny creatures in the soil break down waste and dead animals, returning nutrients to the earth.

What's for dinner, Mr. Wolf?!

All wolves are **carnivores**, meaning they love meat; but they're not picky eaters! A wolf's menu changes depending on where it lives and what the season is. Wolves chow down on a variety of animals, and sometimes even fruits, too!

Large prey

Elk, deer and other large mammals are a wolf's favorite meal. Wolves have to work as a team to catch them.

Sometimes wolves eat fish and even munch on berries, especially when their usual food is scarce.

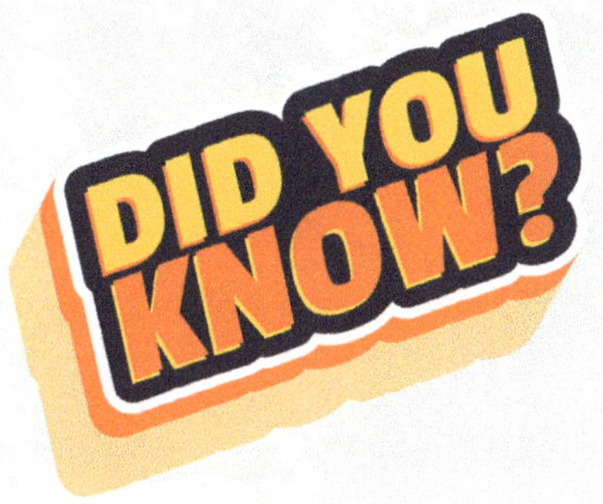

DID YOU KNOW?

Wolves can eat up to 20 pounds of food in one go. That's like eating 80 hamburgers in a single meal!

Medium prey

Smaller animals such as rabbits, marmots and beavers are also on the wolf's menu. These fast animals are hard to catch, so they keep wolves on their toes!

Hunting Techniques

Wolves are talented stalkers. They move with stealth and purpose, using the natural landscape to help them. Whether it's by tracking scent trails or moving silently through the bushes, wolves know how to close in on their prey without being detected.

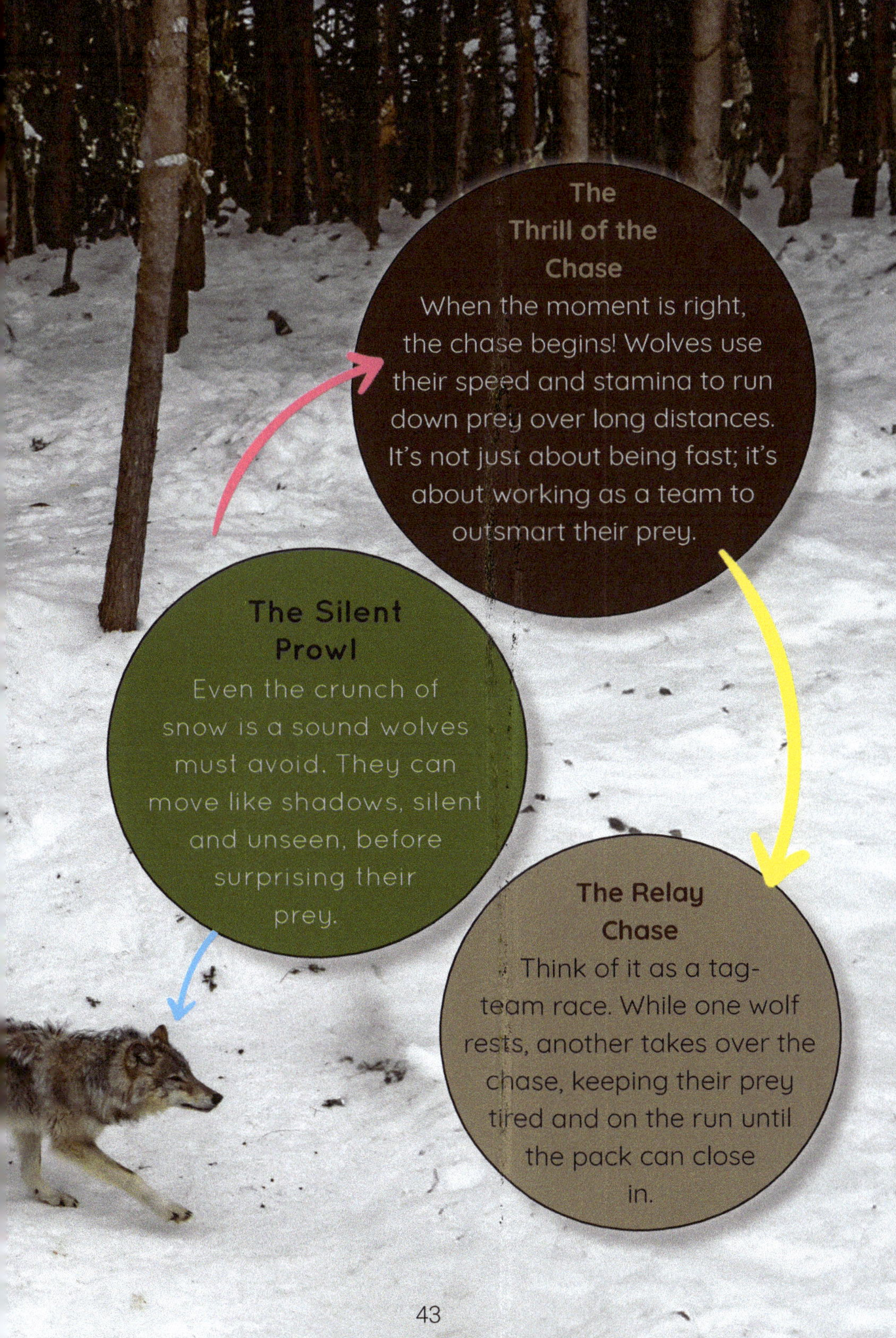

The
Thrill of the
Chase
When the moment is right, the chase begins! Wolves use their speed and stamina to run down prey over long distances. It's not just about being fast; it's about working as a team to outsmart their prey.

The Silent Prowl
Even the crunch of snow is a sound wolves must avoid. They can move like shadows, silent and unseen, before surprising their prey.

The Relay Chase
Think of it as a tag-team race. While one wolf rests, another takes over the chase, keeping their prey tired and on the run until the pack can close in.

Wolves & Humans

Wolves have shared the world with humans for thousands of years, weaving their way into our stories and ecosystems. From the mysterious howls echoing in the night inspiring countless myths to their key role in maintaining healthy landscapes, wolves have been both feared and admired.

In this chapter, we'll discover ancient legends and learn how, in modern times, wolves and humans can live side by side. As we dive into their stories and our shared history, we'll see why wolves are essential to nature and how we can help protect their future.

?!

Did you know...

Some cultures once believed
that wolves were the protectors
of the forests, which isn't far
from the truth. As top predators,
wolves actually help keep
forest ecosystems healthy by
managing the populations of
other animals.

Wolves in Fiction, Mythology & Folklore

Step into a world where wolves wander through wild tales and ancient myths. These creatures have been seen as wise guides, magical beings, and wild spirits of nature.

The Big, Bad Wolf....

From ancient tales to the stories by the Brothers Grimm, wolves have been the stars of many adventures. They teach us to be clever and watch out for tricks.

Think of Little Red Riding Hood's wolf, a sneaky character that shows us why it's important to stick to what we know and stay safe.

Fenrir

In Norse myths, Fenrir is a mighty wolf, so strong that the gods had to tie him up!

Fables with Morals

Do you know the story of The Boy Who Cried Wolf? This fable warns us that if you lie, people might not believe you when you're telling the truth!

Romulus & Remus

According to an old Roman story, two brothers who founded the city of Rome were once cared for by a kind she-wolf.

Living Side-by-Side

Wolves are wild and wonderful, but sometimes living close to humans can create tricky situations!

Wolves and humans sometimes want to hang out in the same places, which can cause a problem. Hungry wolves might visit a farm for a snack, but farmers aren't happy when that snack is their livestock!

?!

Did you know...

Just like you learn to stop and look both ways before crossing the street, wolves in certain areas get used to the sounds of cars and can learn the best times to safely cross roads!

'Wildways' or wildlife corridors are like highways for wolves, letting them travel safely without meeting humans.

Some farmers use animals like guard dogs, donkeys, or even llamas to protect livestock without harming the wolves.

These methods respect the wolves' presence while protecting livestock. That way, wolves contribute to the ecosystem without causing trouble for farmers!

Fences are a simple way for farmers to protect their livestock by keeping wolves out.

Protecting wolves

CONSERVATION

Conservation is all about protecting our planet's amazing animals and the places they call home. Just like we need a cozy house to live in, animals like wolves need safe places to roam, hunt, and raise their pups. But sometimes, wolves face tough challenges that make survival tricky—like losing their homes to growing towns or struggling to find enough food.

But don't worry, there are ways that **you** can help!

?!
Did you know...
Conservationists use a special list to keep track of how animals are doing. When an animal is in danger of vanishing from the wild, it is called 'Endangered'.

ENDANGERED OR SAFE?

Let's explore the journey of wildlife conservation! Look at the path below. Just like in a game, animals can move up and down this path depending on how safe they are in the wild. Our actions can help them stay away from the danger zone of 'Extinct'.

EXTINCT

Golden toad

EXTINCT IN THE WILD

Hawaiian crow

Amur leopard

CRITICALLY ENDANGERED

Did you know...
9,760 animals are currently listed as critically endangered!

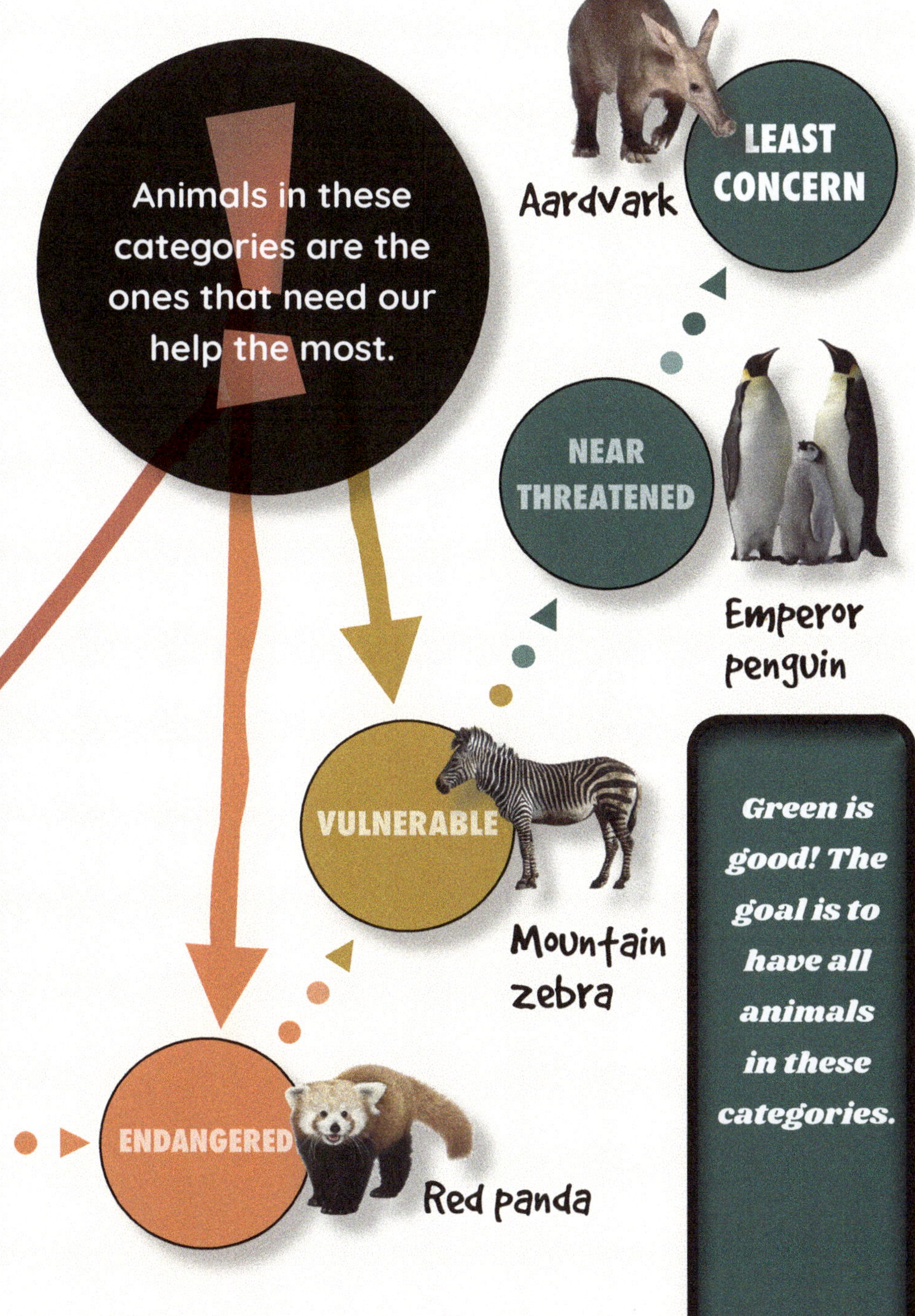

Animals in these categories are the ones that need our help the most.
Aardvark
LEAST CONCERN
NEAR THREATENED
Emperor penguin
VULNERABLE
Mountain zebra
Green is good! The goal is to have all animals in these categories.
ENDANGERED
Red panda

Wolves in Danger

Wolves are amazing animals, but they need our help! Many wolves are struggling to survive because they don't have enough safe space to live and find food. Taking care of their habitats and ensuring a balanced ecosystem is critical for their future.

The Red Wolf

CRITICALLY ENDANGERED

The red wolf used to roam southeastern United States. Now, there are fewer than 40 left in the wild! They're struggling because they're losing their homes and sometimes they have pups with coyotes, which can make it hard for them to survive.

The Mexican Wolf

ENDANGERED

This wolf, native to Mexico and the southwestern United States, is in a tough spot. Their numbers are down because of too much hunting and not enough wild space to call home.

The Ethiopian Wolf

ENDANGERED

As the most endangered carnivore in Africa, the Ethiopian wolf calls the high mountains home. With only about 500 left, they face big challenges like diseases and losing their mountain homes.

What's being done to help wolves?

Community education

Teaching people about wolves and their role in the ecosystem helps to reduce conflicts.

Research & monitoring

Scientists track wolves using technology such as GPS collars to understand how they live.

Gray wolves were one of the first animals to be put on the U.S. Endangered Species list in 1973.

Restoring habitats

Conservationists are also protecting natural habitats. This means planting trees, creating wildlife corridors, and even removing roads to give wolves the space they need to live and hunt.

Wolf conservation agencies

Captive breeding programs

Special centers breed endangered wolves in safe environments. Pups, like these ones in the picture, are cared for by experts until they can be introduced to the wild.

What can _you_ do to help?

Everyone can play a role in ensuring a brighter future for wolves.

Here are some ways you can contribute to their conservation and become a true Wolf Hero!

Share your knowledge

Tell your friends and family about what you've learned about wolves. The more people know about wolves, the more they'll want to help!

Conservation Challenge!

Keep a **conservation diary** this week and write down any action you take that helps the environment, like recycling, saving water, or learning about local wildlife.

Visit a wildlife sanctuary

Support wolf conservation by visiting a wildlife sanctuary. Your visit can help fund the care and protection of wolves.

Become a habitat helper

Join local efforts to preserve and restore natural habitats where wolves live. Planting trees and cleaning up local parks can make a big difference.

Support conservation groups

Many organizations work hard to protect wolves. You can help by raising money with a bake sale, volunteering, or even adopting a wolf online!

Wolf Fun Facts

You've already learned so much about wolves, but there's still much more to discover! Prepare to dive into a treasure trove of even more fascinating and fun facts about wolves.

Playtime or practice? These wolves aren't just having fun — they're honing their skills for hunting and communication within the pack!

Wolves can run at
speeds of up to
38 miles per
hour for short
bursts while
chasing prey.

• • •

Wolves have a
special layer of
fur that keeps them warm in
temperatures as low as -40
degrees Fahrenheit.

• • •

A wolf pack's territory can be as
large as 1,000 square miles, which is
about the size of some cities!

Wolves don't actually howl at
the moon – they use howling to
communicate with other wolves.

• • •

Each wolf has a unique howl, kind of
like a fingerprint, which helps them
identify each other.

• • •

Baby wolves are called **pups**, and a
group of pups born at the same time
is called a **litter**.

• • •

Wolves have 42 teeth, and their
powerful jaws can generate 1,500
pounds of pressure per square inch!

Wolf
pups are
born both blind
and deaf, relying
on their sense of
smell to connect to
their mother and
siblings.

The alpha wolves are the leaders of
the pack and usually the only ones to
have pups.

• • •

Wolves have been living on Earth for
over 300,000 years.

• • •

Wolves have an amazing sense of
smell, which is about 100 times greater
than humans.

• • •

Wolves use body language, like
facial expressions and postures, to
communicate.

A wolf's tail position often tells you its
status in the pack – higher-ranking
wolves hold their tails higher.

• • •

Black fur on a wolf is actually a genetic
trait that came from dogs, likely due to
cross-breeding many years ago.

• • •

When wolves want to play, they do
a little dance called a "play bow",
where they lower their front
bodies and wag their tails,
signaling a friendly
invitation to play
together.

Wolf pups are always born with blue eyes. After around six weeks they change into their adult color.

• • •

Some wolves in the Arctic are white to blend in with the snow and sneak up on their prey.

• • •

There are rare coastal wolves living on Vancouver Island in Canada, whose diet is about 90% seafood! Their favorite food? Salmon.

• • •

Wolves can swim long distances, up to 8 miles (13 km), to find food or new territory.

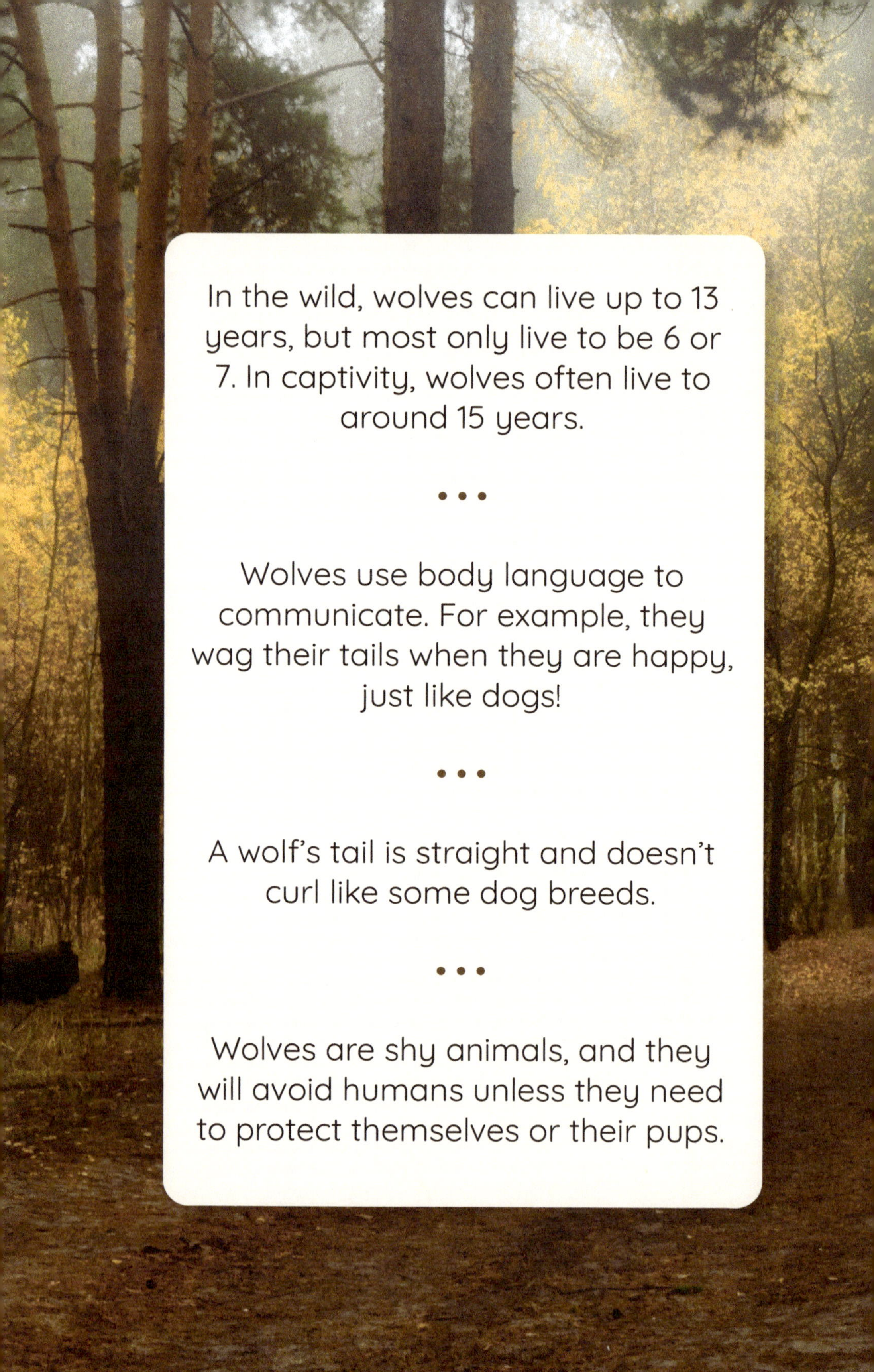

In the wild, wolves can live up to 13 years, but most only live to be 6 or 7. In captivity, wolves often live to around 15 years.

• • •

Wolves use body language to communicate. For example, they wag their tails when they are happy, just like dogs!

• • •

A wolf's tail is straight and doesn't curl like some dog breeds.

• • •

Wolves are shy animals, and they will avoid humans unless they need to protect themselves or their pups.

The biggest wolf ever recorded weighed 227 pounds (103 kg) – that's as much as a heavyweight boxer!

• • •

Wolves can make lots of different sounds, including barks, whines, growls, and, of course, howls.

• • •

A wolf's spine is very flexible, which helps them to make sharp turns when they're running.

In the fall, wolves living in cold areas
grow a second layer of fur to help keep
them warm during the winter.

• • •

Wolves don't sweat; they pant to cool
down when they get hot.

• • •

In some cultures, wolves are seen as
wise and powerful spirit guides.

• • •

Unlike most mammals, wolves can see
blue color.

• • •

Wolves' teeth are not just for eating;
they also use them to carry their pups
around.

The average number of pups in a litter is 4-5, however, it can be up to 10!

• • •

A young wolf may leave its birth pack to start a new pack or join an existing one, a journey called dispersal.

• • •

Wolves have padded feet which act like built-in snow boots to help them walk on snow.

• • •

The red wolf is one of the world's most endangered canids.

• • •

Some wolves can climb trees if the branches are sturdy and low enough.

Wolves use their tails to cover their noses and keep warm when they sleep in cold environments.

• • •

A wolf pack may have a specific trail they use for hunting and traveling, kind of like a forest highway.

• • •

A wolf's paw print is larger than a dog's and has a distinctive pattern that experts can use to track them.

Wolf dens are often reused for several generations.

In fairy tales, wolves often get a bad rap, but they're usually shy and try to avoid people.

When wolves greet each other, they often lick each other's faces - just like we might hug a friend!

Each wolf pack has its own howling language, which members can recognize even at a distance.

• • •

Wolves' fur is a great insulator; it's so effective that snow won't melt on their coat, even if they lie still for hours.

• • •

Once wolves choose a mating partner, they will usually stay with them for the rest of their lives.

• • •

When wolf pups are born, they're not able to see or hear, and they depend on their mother's warmth and milk.

Wolves have an extraordinary sense of smell and can detect other animals, humans, or food items from miles away.

• • •

Despite some spooky stories, wolves are actually not much of a danger to humans; there have only been two fatal attacks in North America in the last century!

• • •

In Latin, "wolf" is "lupus," and in Italian, it's "lupo." These words are the roots for the scientific name for wolves, **Canis lupus**.

The Wolf Quiz

Were you paying attention?! It's time to test your new wolf knowledge!

1   What do you call a group of wolves?

2   How do wolves communicate with each other?

3   What are baby wolves called?

4   Name two subspecies of wolves found in North America.

5   True or False: Wolves can run up to 35 miles per hour.

6   What color are a wolf's eyes when they are born?

7   What is the average number of pups in a wolf litter?

8   What is the average size of a wolf pack?

9   How many teeth do wolves have?

10   Can wolves swim? Yes or No?

11   What's the main prey for wolves in the wild?

12 What do you call the leader of a wolf pack?

13 True or False: All wolves howl at the moon.

14 How do wolves mark their territory?

15 Name a continent where wolves <u>don't</u> live in the wild.

16 What's the scientific name for the gray wolf?

17 What special hair feature helps wolves stay warm?

18 How far can a wolf's howl be heard?

19   True or False: Wolves have padded feet to sneak up on prey silently.

20   What do wolves typically do before they start hunting?

21   What unique family role do older wolves in the pack sometimes take on?

22   Do wolves eat fish? Yes or No?

23   What do wolves do to greet each other?

Answers

1. A pack
2. Through howls, body language, and scent marking
3. Pups
4. Gray wolf (Canis lupus), Red wolf (Canis rufus)
5. True
6. Blue
7. 4-5
8. 5 to 8 members
9. 42
10. Yes
11. Large mammals (like deer, elk, and moose)
12. Alpha
13. False

14.   By urinating or leaving scents from their body

15.   Antarctica, Australasia

16.   Canis lupus

17.   A double coat of fur

18.   Up to 10 miles in open terrain

19.   True

20.   They often circle and scent mark

21.   Babysitters or mentors to the pups

22.   Yes

23.   They lick each other's faces

Can you find all the words below in
the word search puzzle on the right?

PACK   TERRITORY   FOREST

HOWL   PUP   CARNIVORE

ALPHA   HUNTERS   ARCTIC

Wolves

WORD SEARCH

```
F  C  A  R  N  I  V  O  R  E  H  G
D  S  P  A  C  K  Q  W  F  T  A  D
H  C  Z  B  R  D  F  O  R  E  S  T
U  U  W  D  F  C  C  B  R  R  J  J
T  U  N  T  R  C  T  X  C  R  Y  Y
E  Y  T  T  S  H  X  I  U  I  T  R
B  K  Y  U  E  N  O  B  C  T  E  S
Z  F  S  D  F  R  T  W  E  O  D  D
C  S  X  P  Y  H  S  E  L  R  D  F
V  D  A  L  P  H  A  R  B  Y  A  V
E  F  C  X  U  N  J  F  S  E  C  Z
S  A  S  D  P  V  J  D  F  R  X  Z
```

Solution

	C	A	R	N	I	V	O	R	E		
		P	A	C	K				T		
H				R		F	O	R	E	S	T
	U				C				R		
		N			T				R		
			T		H		I		I		
			E		O		C	T			
				R		W		O			
				S		I		L	R		
		A	L	P	H	A			Y		
			U								
			P								

Sources

What's in a name? Why we call them painted wolves. (n.d.). Retrieved from https://www.bbcearth.com/news/whats-in-a-name-why-we-call-them-painted-wolves

Wolf Anatomy - Body Types & Fur. (2023). Retrieved from https://animalcorner.org/wolf-anatomy/

Red Wolf. (n.d.). Retrieved from https://www.nwf.org/Educational-Resources/Wildlife-Guide/Mammals/Red-Wolf

Red Wolf. (n.d.). Retrieved from https://kids.nationalgeographic.com/animals/mammals/facts/red-wolf

Arctic Wolves: Diet, Habitat, Threats & Other Facts. (n.d.). Retrieved from https://www.ifaw.org/animals/arctic-wolf

Northern Rocky Mountain wolf. (n.d.). Retrieved from https://animalia.bio/northern-rocky-mountain-wolf

The first-ever IUCN assessment of the Himalayan Wolf is out. And it is grim. (n.d.). Retrieved from https://www.downtoearth.org.in/news/wildlife-biodiversity/the-first-ever-iucn-assessment-of-the-himalayan-wolf-is-out-and-it-is-grim-93852

The ambigious taxonomy of the elusive Himalayan Wolves. (2023). Retrieved from https://thinkwildlifefoundation.com/the-ambigious-taxonomy-of-the-elusive-himalayan-wolves/

Arabian Wolf (Canis lupus arabs). (2020). Retrieved from https://thewolfintelligencer.com/arabian-wolf-canis-lupus-arabs/

The Return of the Wolf in Europe: Working Towards Coexistence. (n.d.). Retrieved from https://rewildingeurope.com/rewilding-in-action/wildlife-comeback/wolf/

Pacific Wild. (2023). Wolves and the Food Web. Retrieved from https://pacificwild.org/wolves-and-the-food-web/

Hungry as a Wolf: What Wolves Eat: International Wolf Center. (2023). Retrieved from https://wolf.org/wolf-info/basic-wolf-info/biology-and-behavior/hunting-feeding-behavior/hungry-as-a-wolf-what-wolves-eat/

Costello, G. (2021). A Legacy of Connecting the Missing Links for Wildlife. Retrieved from https://www.wildlandsnetwork.org/news/a-legacy-of-connecting-the-missing-links-for-wildlife

Nosowitz, D. (2021). How Can Farmers Coexist With Wolves? Retrieved from https://modernfarmer.com/2021/09/farmers-ranchers-wolves/

Conserving the Mexican Wolf: U.S. Fish & Wildlife Service. (2024). Retrieved from https://www.fws.gov/program/conserving-mexican-wolf

Ethiopian Wolf. (n.d.). Retrieved from https://www.awf.org/wildlife-conservation/ethiopian-wolf

Wolf FAQs & Answers: International Wolf Center. (2023). Retrieved from https://wolf.org/wolf-info/basic-wolf-info/wolf-faqs/

Gray Wolf Biology. Retrieved from https://fwp.mt.gov/binaries/content/assets/fwp/conservation/wildlife-reports/wolf/qandasgraywolfbiology.pdf
Wolf Species Have "Howling Dialects." (2016). Retrieved from https://nywolf.org/2016/12/wolf-species-have-howling-dialects/

Evolution of the wolf. (2024). Retrieved from https://en.wikipedia.org/wiki/Evolution_of_the_wolf

Learn about black wolves: International Wolf Center. (2024). Retrieved from https://wolf.org/original-articles/learn-about-black-wolves/

Body language of wolves. (2019). Retrieved from https://www.livingwithwolves.org/body-language-of-wolves/

Petri, A. E. (2016). Meet the Rare Swimming Wolves That Eat Seafood. Retrieved from https://www.nationalgeographic.com/animals/article/sea-oceans-wolves-animals-science

Gray Wolf. (n.d.). Retrieved from https://www.nwf.org/Educational-Resources/Wildlife-Guide/Mammals/Gray-Wolf

Largest canid. (n.d.). Retrieved from https://www.guinnessworldrecords.com/world-records/76255-largest-canid

Gray Wolf Identification. (2022). Retrieved from https://westernwildlife.org/gray-wolf-canis-lupus/library-2/

Monty, & Monty), M. A. (nickname. (2023). What colors do Wolves see? Wolves Color & Night Vision Explained (Updated). Retrieved from https://howitsee.com/what-colors-do-wolves-see/

Wolf Facts. (n.d.). Retrieved from https://www.california-wolfcenter.org/wolf-facts

Wolf Dens. (n.d.). Retrieved from http://www.wolfcountry.net/information/WolfDen.html

How do wolves keep warm? (n.d.) Retrieved from https://www.wolf.org/wp-content/uploads/2018/02/WildKids_spring2018.pdf

Howl you doing?!

As we reach the end of our epic adventure through the wild world of wolves, we hope you've enjoyed discovering these majestic creatures as much as we've loved bringing their stories to you.

Your thoughts are incredibly valuable to us, so we would be over the moon if you could leave a review where you picked up this book.

Your insights and experiences will aid other young explorers in uncovering the thrilling world of wolves and inspire us to keep creating content that's both enlightening and enjoyable for all.

Thank you for being part of our pack!

ALSO BY JENNY KELLETT

... and more!

Available at
www.bellanovabooks.com

and all major online bookstores.

www.ingramcontent.com/pod-product-compliance
Lightning Source LLC
LaVergne TN
LVHW051111180726
843512LV00011B/792

9 782487 191105